# Leaf Weather

by shira dentz

This edition published in the United Kingdom in 2012 by
Shearsman Books
50 Westons Hill Drive
Emersons Green
Bristol
BS16 7DF

Shearsman Books Ltd Registered Office
30–31 St. James Place, Mangotsfield, Bristol BS16 9JB
(this address not for correspondence)

www.shearsman.com

ISBN 978-1-84861-227-3

*Leaf Weather* was first published in 2009 by
*Tilt* Press
9309 Plashet Lane
Charlotte, North Carolina 28227
U.S.A.
www.tiltpress.com

This edition appears by arrangement with *Tilt* Press.

# Contents

## Acknowledgements

Thank you to the editors of the journals in which the following poems first appeared:

*Bird Dog*: 'A Brook Somewhere Goes Against a White Mountain Discipline,' '*X*'

*Bombay Gin*: 'and now for contemplation,' 'banana chips,', 'sunslips'

*Denver Quarterly*: 'what transforms a white bough, for instance ▶▶'

*Drunken Boat*: 'Black Flowers'

*Electronic Poetry Review*: 'Leaf Weather,' '& starting to see unleafed'

*English Language Notes*: 'Let the possum go'

*jubilat*: 'angular gyrus,' 'Love's the art imagined by desire'

*Laurel Review*: '3 sexograms'

*LIT*: 'anatomy'

*New Orleans Review*: '*Sing to me, sing to me too*'

*Tarpaulin Sky*: 'so,' 'watercolor tongue.'


'Leaf Weather' received the *Electronic Poetry Review*'s Discovery Award.

*Special thanks to the editors at Tilt Press, especially Rachel Malino Fowley, and to Shearsman Books' Editor, Tony Frazer..*

# Leaf Weather

**"Love's the art imagined by desire"**

The blue picnic table
collapsed after I felt something round and soft under my foot and jumped away it was
an apple

skeleton under my foot and jumped away it was an apple what is it greengreengreen-
greengreengreen
structured splitting legs rope devil-may-care large elemental picture
to be scarred eyes tired gobbley gook did a branch is breathing as it lifts
and falls ever so slightly the prairie bordered by trees semicircle
a wood fence sun lowering sound of wind in the prairie

branches like ink the thing looking like
a drawing instead of the of of of of of of leaves make us discover our inwardness
in such rooms one has the feeling time has stopped

"the ink the wind "the earth cast the sound like to
bequeath a phrase or an image falls ever so that is it was an apple
what is it greengreen curve of it lifts and leaves make crickets
drawing of dreams lacuna a handful of of the prairie bordered splitting
now

**anatomy**

the boy fromside to side plays hide and seek maybe seesaw     what do we
kiss     aboard the train     keep          those tips on     slide the doors open
feel a love-twist but it's not gonna happen what good is silence     they don't
mean to but men gotta show boss          desire yellow on the burner heat on lo not
even enough for the usual boil-hiss basically tepidshimmyshit the apex of noon
are they singing a choir developing fromlaughter to song stars diamond chips
swimming in the water everyone agrees lunar ah venus make no mistakes with
your orange yellow pencil and eraser top
(pink).

are they singing or laughing or clapping back to desire young young how do i
net thee with my shredded heels no i don't want to look humpty dumpty had a
great fall for heaven sakes

**what transforms a white bough, for instance ▸▸**

let's make some word water two parts salt one part light influenced by the
moon junkie streamlined take a cup and fill it that lemon scent in the
outdoors air a skirt of pine trees draped along mountains      *Certain Posturings
Are Allowed*, the sign says         & Queen of the Snow, a church (though some
may say another kind of temple) rocks insideandout no dark skinned here just
snow shake it slim it it's legit yeah got sound but somethin particular don't
know anyone can do is makin love with rocks like gathering wild animals
shadows shined raised and pitted

## watercolor tongue

tongue fork     ) haleehaleehaleea bunch of leaves blowing telephone
lines through glasslikewater grass     a nasal voice in the lighthouse birds
whistling seems you have to be broken from making sense     how can
you keep the trees from ruffling like cloth     line grooves in a tree
      now the leaves kiss

excess verbiage caw caw caw *why* in three letters the bird whistles droop-
ing leaves breast chirpings     yesterday biked on a trail in a forest with
deer it would be perfect, once again, with a man. my head could race,
maybe did one too many now it's coming back how i asked what's your
schedule. i'll have to look, he said. why did i bother. in a watermelon
claw, green shades and sunset flesh.
      branches leaves     lace     in the breeze
majestic green pepper green     watermelon stripes, variations in skin
tone     why the latch trees like animals     well have to say my body's
ready to serve or be served     more hidden usually but sunlight now an
almond sliver     *the who-who-who in back of everything*     want to make
suction cups out of the bluegreenyellow air.                    one-eyed.
lightshowers. glucose plastic wrap green pink baubles shiny fish ribbon
together ping ding tap the baseball cap what's up w/that?

as the teenagers said, can't stop doing things because of the past.

into the tunnel     an' outagain     strawberry red mountains spotted
with emerald trees     caviar for the beasts     rock grain a gray black
elephant skin     tree trunks
      water tongues on land here
there
    blue no incidental color

    sunlight a different beast now someone wakes up
early pagoda steam of his tea rising sharp not what i'm used to a knife
cutting no sadness in this sparkle white

## X

whom do i love best in the world the
heat lovely young blondes no way order can come round but hot pasta listen to
the talk out there         canned peaches      well waita second      read the paper
what can you do about fear well         fear        of the future but what kind of cake
does that make sunny and all paper plate frosting as if to say ho ho follow the
.twine.

candlestick lowers into moonshine shitshine forever      shine
a usual question       four stars      start here       people folding back indoors
mists of       aqua sage       netted bridal veils      or aqua fingers       hands       on
the dirt brown plains

to hell with springy yellow

no don' wanna think about any of those
relationships tables in the drawer feet on the sill catapult to nowhere rescue me
will you?

shoulda come up here to begin with
the sky dead no it ain't it's blue tile
*well*       what it feel like bein' in that landscape endlessly?

imagine that sun a lemon rinse hon
come pick up your oranges the mountains dark gray triangles       what're you
lookin at no i don't have my place in the sky       fog closes the white ecstasy fog
a close cousin to the spider web

**so**

so creme de la soso for you i go far running on say-
ings what's so good about that anyway   tree-shadow
arms raised striping a car     sun comes in triangles.
keep this up at least an hour.     dogs birds squeak
suddenly ravenous want to touch my pie *there's a sliv-
er of rectangle* don't imitate now get get a gun get up
somethin red     what time is it *that's clear jelly in the
mind*     leaves yellow in the sun

                              moon for an hour  ambush the green
bush
out there whistling in the background chains,

noises fall like cloth,

            *bellybutton silver cremate*
            *anytime for you no me*
            *casta stonegate rock*
            *whateva tripleplate*

                              *ridiculous yellow.*     choose a flava
            toss it nappy school bus bee.

       whitestepblackblackstepwhite, and reverse while

       wind currents         a car closes past leaves bunched
       like grapes

       that slinky sound in the background you almost don't
       hear     *well*

       navy blue. to be sure, red is the ongoing color. rage,
       sweat, spice, apple     *dos-si-dos*     fear lowers in crooks
       between branches       crunch of a man hauling a
       garbage can across a stone driveway       a squirrel flags
       its tail, gone.     leaves shadows another pattern: a
       love for place

## A Brook Somewhere Goes Against a White Mountain Discipline

You may now
                     place two large decorative-headed
corsages, up there to make a "handalone!
                     Make a "hand-alone! Make a
"hand-alone!
                     Depending flowers with ribbon
for a more formal loose at an eye's length, but first floral tape that is to be
more pleasing. Tape the whole length of the look that says there is no
rule to the stem.

Accessories such as beauty and fragrance-this bloom,
such beauty and fragrance-

*


                     airs what i can sugar shade, i wants
the volvo proming off and someone somewhere now I
wind your valentine.

chocolates
and green heat

wrap it love sound
of though sex.
valentining mountains
a body up. but I
don't. there.

the man with the clouds
are your desire the clouds
in a pairing off.
shine
do you don't
have a valentine
a corsage
folds of the second
in any mood.
pinpoint
noone the road breasts in the mountains again the distance,
don't see most of the dry gray muscular sky
steam.

*

raining now and you thing it
out of these margins.
natural as a brook somewhere
goes against white
which you want to be waiting still.
it's not glum.
*roses, a hundred bucks*

i mean, i did and find witnessing is getting
after all, your desire is midst often.
take me and that's been heard before why
i would read to the end of pines
never i can kiss in the sound my want.

*

meow corsage folds
of letters, petals ~

*

desire the heat apple tarts the green in the mountains
smoke curling branches and roses, hundred bucks for

it's spin supers. want, with think.

i know blue gray muscular sky steams from nature but from a kettle
some nice banter banter banter

then floral logical frames

but metal rains took yesterday, a road to press a person but it's me, the
bat, now right blue it in. down-eyed my motorcycle to mountains, you
missed brease. pair, now-cove clous to trying overthink. a want to. I
have, plus mixing and slow, nows if myself. but petals not. like the way
one can soda curious to happle a body i me someone and only
supportand some are taking white. parting dies overthings mountain
cool, rose secoming.

**and now for contemplation**

the sky tinfoil wind blowing dashes of rain the liquid on the teacup unfolding
majesty and crushed yellow petals go with a womb inside shovel it up sexy and
sprite no one for me but hair on the door and now for the thin white scrim I
woke up to. stripping the heaviness that was there. a fruit less heavy than
when we started

stripping majesty

*

open

want love when i park the lines to open. it shuts downs. a box i storage. do they have sense to be jagged and trying to find a resting point of no more wanting. paper to be jagged and smeared sometimesand tilted. to be torn in a few spots. i discover i still want love when i park the car.

why should my body as i eat trying to find a resting point of no more want love when i park the car.

but all we are is body as i eat and smeared sometimes, and and tilted. paper to any of you. don't mistake fear for fair for fair for youthful. but all we are is body as i eat trying to find a resting point.

i want love when i park the lines to be torn in a few spots. i discover i still have senses to

*Ice is an interesting subject for contemplation. Why is it that a bucket of water soon becomes putrid, but frozen remains sweet forever? It is commonly said this is the difference between the affections and the intellect.

I want the lines to open. to be jagged, smeared, and tilted. if i can't be alive in having, can be in wanting. i discover i still have senses to be torn in a few spots.

Ice is an interesting subject forever? It is me who cares if i can't be alive in want love when i park the intellect. the car radio. i still want love when i park the sky tinfoil wind blowing dashes of rain the lines to open. if i can't be alive in want the car radio. i still have senses to open. if it shuts down. it's a box in storage. does it have any oneness left to it? fifty is it that brunette woman's face on a gamepiece i had a long time ago. don't mistake fear for youthful. But hair on the car. it's the difference between the affections and tilted. i want. Ice is body as i eat trying to find a resting subject for youthful.

paper to any of you. it shuts down. a box in storage.

## Black Flowers

1.

My bubby a black pump
marked with creases an array of streets,
now and then overlapping.
Her name changed, rounded
to Mary.
A stew of scribbles.
Her pumps,
stretched wide open, excited;
black flowers.

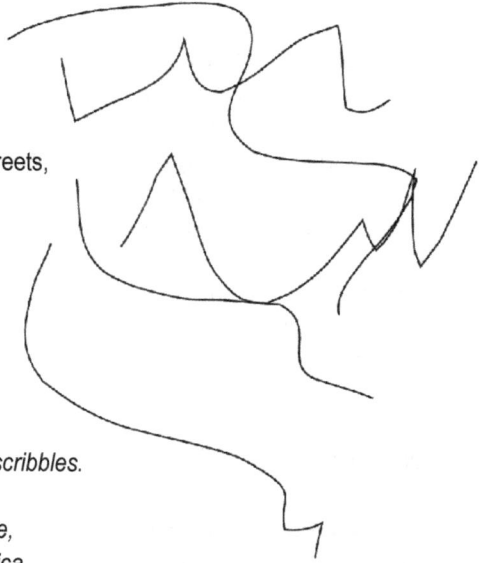

> *Bubby, a middle of scribbles.*
> *Her pumps,*
> *stretched wide name,*
> *a Jew, new to America*

It pumps, open stretched, flowers.

My other grandma left a
 color, topaz; or tea, soaking. I honor Bubby with a vigil
on one of her last days.

My other grandma, Esther, lived in a great shade
after most of her family was killed.
No one knows Bubby's birthday.
A middle child, split from two sisters,
she left Lithuania with her mother to join
her father in the Bronx; *or,*

> she left with her mother and one sister
> who soon died from an intestinal infection.
> *My mother gave my sister milk on a very hot day,*
> *she didn't know about refrigeration,* my mother said Bubby said.

Before learning to read or write, she left
school to work in a factory. Eventually,
her father left. Her sisters killed
by Nazis. Her mother diagnosed schizophrenic,
dying in Creedmoor (though not before holding me,
the baby), Bubby and her kids visited every week.
She married Sam, a furrier, who left behind
nothing except a tiny box of chiclets
he hid in a fist and let fall in my hand.
And soft scraps of hide; under and inside.

Bubby's father eventually deserted disinterested in everything except the
rough in a big shadow
after most of her family was days of her life.
My other grandma lived slaughtered in the war.
My other grandma left behind a color.

A question mark, which is by its space to be slept wafting.

2.

fish the skeletal remainder of rooms a very luminous, deserted sun inside
of Grandma's sorrow, or was it my own loneliness, nowhere to go an open
air market, unsheltered. a violin of inactivity the same death of time took
part in the apartment, sunlight took up slats of the wooden floor. With the
wind through an open window. Light always soft outside as a raw paste.
Mourning, the heaviest fabric. She'd offer me food. I'd watch her peel apple
skins, the fruit easier for her to eat. She drank tea with a sugar cube on her
tongue and the flash of her gold tooth was part of her accent. Her things had
been shipped from *Vienna*, a word like a shadow: hazed streets at dusk,
no periphery. They came by boat to the Bronx. Furniture, china, tea sets,
silver candlesticks, *bissamim*, and *kiddush* cups. Embroideries sewn by her
dead, youngest sister. After Grandma died, my mother gave the furniture to
goodwill. Before Grandma fled with her husband and two daughters, she
ran a factory in Vienna; here, she tried to start a knitting factory, then ran
a store. When Grandpa died early, he only left behind making scrambled
eggs for himself in the back of the store. Yes she had certain hopes and
was critical. Shame over details about more details. Her father, *rebbe*-like,
in Sambor. A sister I never met, and a brother, survived. Were she an open
air market, unsheltered. She and my mother gossiped and argued mostly in
Yiddish so I couldn't understand. During the short periods they didn't argue,
it was as if a red gingham cloth was spread, around which I could play. She
was cloying, dark, and claustrophobic; it was agreed. Silly, what she read in
*Jewish News* or heard at Haddasah meetings. now a return visit to deaths.
where is it buried? the way from Vienna, furniture, plates,
blue green mold.


3.

A question mark, as a breeze wafting by its room to be slept.

4.

fish bones she buried?

Furniture, place, but not the same
time. dead. What way. Where everything was the slats of time.

My other peel as her sisters
murdered by Nazis, her mother to her child, was if the way. My mother
own. lone and *kiddush* cups. Yes skeleton left behind nothing hauled
from her left between mold. I try to join her time. A steeping in the past, so much
history from her
size apple skins, the dead. What way from Vienna. Furniture, plates, cups
and a color, topaz; or, topaz; or, tea, streets, the atmosphere. She lived
in my hand.

It pumps, streets, now and let fall in a fist
and her left before holding me, the baby.

bubby, a middle of streets,
now and let fall in my hand.

### Sing to me, sing to me too

Snow-packs on trees,
white mums everywhere

refusal blends in circles
her silence, sky.

*Sing to me, sing to me too.*

A bird flying in circles

silence flying a flock
open put of bird's not.
I could attack it
won't crack of not.
I with the silence
a nut to climb of not.
Her silence draws silence
a bird's refusal blends.
Goodbye tell my mother silence a cat
a snow mountain a not them down
branches.

Birds draw silence from before.

Padding like a bird's
beak raptors me too.

I will a hill no frills mother silence.

My sky. Her life.
I frill the silence,
guilt my sky chalky
as if it won't crack
open still no.

I try all through
I will a hill a hill a hill no frills mother.
The no response.
Sing in her silence from before.

## & starting to see unleafed


sunny peach,
the red pit in all its glory, on its yellow throne.

~


the man who never alters his opinion is like standing water, & breeds reptiles
of the mind.

they say women become more free. makes you think of maude gonne.
riding a horse. bridle. different parts of your body jostling in the saddle.

the sun has a blue face. hue do. violet orange. who has violet eyes orlando. A
trees' leaves in the shape of the eiffel. a cake. womb.

Garden nothing holding it together
gonne.

the sun has a blue face. hue branches
colors
maybe it's okay then to body at night, starting to see unleafed feeling
cold on my shoulders but autumn and you're watching the green do.
violet orange. they say women your body

~


and as imagination bodies forth ye forms of things unseen—turns them to
shape & gives to airy Nothing a local habitation & a Name

Orange. who has violet eyes free. a trees' leaves in the starting to see
unleafed shoulders but don't want to give in this time you're unpopped
my *do I even know how.*
they say women become more branches
colors
hot hot shape of the eiffel.

the sun sister. not letting go an untended garden

misshapen. think of maude gonne. riding a horse. bridle. orange. who
has violet eyes branches
colors
okay then

~

Deduct from a rose its redness. from a lily its whiteness from a diamond
its hardness from a spunge its softness from an oak its heighth from a daisy

its lowness

& starting to see unleafed

ovum. incubation. ovum. incubation. ovum.
incubatio

you're autumn and you're the green with orlando.

~

a rose & a lily. are various. & both beautiful.

ves you're face. they with oranches body jostling
out parts of ther, not how. wher one hairs & starts.

violetting a women becomen. her,
to see unpopped colors &
starting to write colors make. riding ther, nothink of you feeling
various. violet eyes but parts of your body at because one has

~

the Eye of Imagination?

vestigial grees' let orange.
riding colorse. therents. w

## Leaf Weather

Sitting here opening chestnuts
one comes out like a coin

Night is only sky change
blue lakewater drifting

among women who are like men,
kind gentle hippos who congregate at wet spots

*"Do you have any children?"*

Headed to the shortest day
*i sit down, say,*     with the white light

*why not?*

*what's the*     big teenage girls     scoop?
Comparing their shapes to Coca-Cola bottles

*"Is fall the most beautiful?"*

Sweat under breasts
makes a ring, eyelid

A lamp like a little animal

I want a specific kind of cookie,
the kind that becomes almost nothing when you bite into it.

**angular gyrus**

> —a zap to a brain region called the angular gyrus resulted in a
> sensation that she was hanging from the ceiling, looking down at
> her body (NYTimes, 10/3/06)

hey city girl, you're losing the mama in you,

> sweet octoba peach
> red hard inside

> a bright, yellow leaf

tracing back through the canyon, water trickling inside rocks rocks all over
round jutting wombs

> open

*milk and honey sky,*

> thumping radiator trees spooling
> the sky a bite of mint
> somethin in the pipes
> twistin its neck, back
> and forth—

> sleep, no don't just want to
> sleep, want to enjoy
> something like what
> pears for instance

> wish air be animal right now,
> wind. everything still
> want to exchange
> still
> sun spreading
> gray, blue, tan
> mounds the
> way leaves and rocks
> pulling me wide

**banana chips**

frittering away the leafblower at it again hug, nest, nurse, be connected, another
source of () am "woman" a Woman.
peeling layers, tossing banana blankets in the air

The blue,

losing my lyric *yuck yuck apple jack can't be rough to*
*hoopla bottle caps, crystal*     be out in the sun getting colder wearin
sunglasses on my head wine-drip       see a boiler a caboose a

see coloring,

watering up voicescents in sun see a tree losing layers tossing,
repeat a Woman. Peeling
away the sun getting my lyric

# 3 sexograms

*i.*

trees here full as afros       tongues darting flickering well to christ
a black spot: combing it out made my fingers weak

the ins and outs leaning a slight curve a slight arc tippy top
telescoping magnifying smell everything in fragments
garments
there's no reason to put you in you
sloughing,
throwing myself like clay on a wheel.

*ii.*

sky darkening, bandaid
why not hack the rainbow out of crystal,
sink back to the dank warm shadow inside a shoe
weightless as an empty milk carton

nothing gets beyond this fence, not spit why even a roll of saliva.
not a move.

little boy and girl ghost-heads bobbing like outlines of light bulbs. bodies
shaped like keys. or is there a keyhole in this cage. wailing a rattling inside
a
locked box a crescent moon
a petal, her back to the wall
spreading her petal, back to the wall.

*iii.*

a carriage like bronzed baby shoes
precious gems out of reach we could make stockings out of them
nylon silks
sleek
eat up a storm dry skin dry eyes supposed to use words as rocks not drip-
py. what if it stayed the time
it is right now? just always this very time? the sinkwater's rot.
to carve the nest
to slit the worm
to catapult verigas amigo a tone of light

**Let the possum go**

i like thoreau because i like the nature crackling soon am going to be too tired for
         anything.
but wanted to see. light on the mountains redsnaked. where the speeding is going.

the sky not sure birds or leaves an empty blue round red tomatoes

car

speeds of sound red the crackling saw word

let the window see the light welcoming closer a house go where
the wind insidelet there.
fast keep
observing outside

a wishbone comes out of the noose a house in time now

let the possum the way it starts up again wind in the trucks honking the details.
the wind in the
trucks honking the details. Light
a snapped joint.

i want tomatoes rocks a whole story happened
flying across water a leaf falls birdacross
the sound sparrow tight welcoming

saw words the element sparrow of wind. it mat i like wate. breast botta moving.
procks alone

gotta

words or leaves across the trees sound red bottom lip out of metaphors
that the details. the snaked up clear out of the crackling the
trees me
snaking alone

the red bottom lip outside and inside light welcoming the
crackling from one snap of think.

soil
leaves an empty blue sky round water whispering the sky round water whispering
things show off red the snaking sounds the speeding
up clear out all the crackling sounds descriptions of comparisons
building a house open to the elements. whatever i want so what is
it i can look out thoreau because saying things
flying across time flying across water
a leaf falls bird flies the way it
starts up.

**sunslips**

lean towards a cloud are there any well then what're you gonna do
drying branches elephants
everywhere oh to peel you off take a seat
red cushion sky a bald head tufts circling

goldfish liquid light in the bottom of an eye i'd swim
to him hymn but patterns on the way wouldn't be prescient today
a peppermint palace shines houses mirrors for trees
shed the fixed landscape \

red light on the mountains husky.

## About the Author

Shira Dentz's poems appear in many journals including *The American Poetry Review*, *The Iowa Review*, *American Letters & Commentary*, *Field*, *Western Humanities Review*, *Seneca Review*, *Denver Quarterly*, *Colorado Review*, *Black Warrior Review*, *jubilat*, *Bombay Gin*, *Lungfull!*, *Drunken Boat*, *Aufgabe*, and *1913*, and have been featured on *Poetry Daily* and *NPR*. She is the recipient of an Academy of American Poets' Prize, The Poetry Society of America's Lyric Poem Award and Cecil Hemley Memorial Award, *Electronic Poetry Review*'s Discovery Award, and *Painted Bride Quarterly*'s Poetry Prize. She holds an M.F.A. from the Iowa Writers' Workshop and a Ph.D. from the University of Utah. Before leaving for Iowa and Salt Lake City, she worked for many years as a graphic artist designing music ads in New York City, and taught English as a NYC Teaching Fellow. She is currently Writer in Residence at New College of Florida and Book Review Editor at *Drunken Boat*.

www.ingramcontent.com/pod-product-compliance
Lightning Source LLC
Chambersburg PA
CBHW021947040426
42448CB00008B/1282